DEPARTURES

ABOUT WHAT HAPPENED, AND MY
TELLING OF IT

I0528523

BY

JOSEPH MILANA

<u>DEDICATION</u>

A memoir of sorts, in part; in part, something else.

ACKNOWLEDGMENTS

What in effect the rest is all about.

TABLE OF CONTENTS

1
EULOGY

It's been a year now since this period of passings began. Over it seems, with no new departures to be seen. But then, how much different was it twelve months ago?

The first was the most disruptive, yet the least important. A professional demise: forced retirement. And if not quite that, if that is I choose to start anew, to relaunch (fortunately not strictly necessary) then, at least for sure, a total separation, a tearing, an "et tu Brute".

But more of all that later.

11/20/23

Rich

The most important came a few months later, nearly equally as sudden: my brother's passing. My brother, the person who, outside my parents, influenced me the most, and perhaps, through the secondary effects he had on my parents themselves, even more so. Early February I received a call from Richie's group home, Richard had been admitted to the local hospital due to chest pains.[1] Initial plans were to insert some stents, but

---

[1] To me he was and always will be Rich or Richie, as I am still Joey to some of my cousins, but at the group home he was Richard; a protocol I had to be careful of, particularly in my conversations with Rich.

his vessels were determined to be too small and clogged for that to be viable. He was thus moved to Camden, New Jersey's premier cardio-center. I flew out the next day, staying with Ronnie and Philip, Lauren's sister and her husband, in Philadelphia. After further tests, including another CAT scan and an MRI, multiple bypass surgery was scheduled. All set to go, that Friday, and then the delay: they wanted to wait to get his numbers down, to get them better before the operation. I had wanted the surgery to get done, knowing its urgency, but also thus, the sooner to get back to Lauren; the less to impose on my in-laws. Now I am grateful for the little extra time the delay gave us.

Except for the days Ronnie was being treated, Philip drove me over The Ben Franklin bridge to visit Richie. Never needed to ask. A good friend, one I didn't know I had. We'd stay a few hours. Because of lingering Covid restrictions, only I was allowed upstairs. We didn't want to be away too long, but I wouldn't leave until I had gotten the latest update from the doctors. And if only Richie said it was okay. Some days that took longer than others. Once, something had gone wrong with a nurse; another, his breakfast, his morning routine, had been interrupted, for a test. One time I arrived and he was in tears, insisting he wanted to leave, that he didn't want the surgery, and that he just wanted "to go home". It was then that I realized that after all the shuffling back and forth, after all the tests, and all the doctor and surgeon visits, he hadn't been clearly told why he was there. The first, knee-jerk thought was to assert authoritatively he had to stay, that he had to have the surgery: period. And I could almost hear my mother saying that. But that would have only worked for her. Richie was my older brother, and officially/legally an independent adult. So instead, I said to him, "okay, it's your decision to stay or go, but", then pausing, "if he left, he would have a heart attack." And that quieted him, immediately digesting what that meant (what he understood always surprised strangers),

"and, I would die"

"yes"

 "then, I better stay."

Rich was fourteen months older than me. My mother said that after they finally brought him home from the hospital, facing a lifetime of health challenges, my father told her, "Let's have another". And thus, I became, I was, I am.

12/18/2023[2]

---

[2] These dates reflect the composition of the first draft of the specified section. Edits are not tracked unless substantial changes were made. Occasionally there are sizable insertions within existing text. All these dates are given in parenthesis. The gap between the first date and this one, the next, occurred because as I was still collecting the mental energy and devotion required for this effort, Lauren and I were both hit over Thanksgiving with Covid (for the very first time). I became sick and then passed it on to Lauren three days later, after testing *negative* with a home kit. When Lauren tested positive, with her being immunocompromised, we promptly had a prescription for paxlovid ordered and filled within 24 hours of her first symptoms. Having started to improve, no longer running a fever, I elected to forego the drug. By the next day she was feeling better. I took noticeably longer. The following week we

When he first came home as an infant, months after being born, after failing to thrive, after all the experts insisting on getting their chance at him, Rich was seen for the first time by our family pediatrician. It was then he was found to have one leg shorter than the other. A simple test, simply extending the two legs, for an ailment not uncommon, and if caught immediately after birth easy to correct, but instead for Rich, after this delay, would require over a year of orthopedic treatment, with his leg and hip in a cast. It was then my mother refused to see any more specialists: Rich was home, he was hers to take care of.

I don't recall Rich in a cast, but he said he did. There are baby pictures of him, laying on his stomach, and instead of like mine when taken at the same age with my head raised, supported by my arms, his head is down, off to the side, laying on his hands. The expression on his face, eyes wide open, he would keep his entire life.

My most vivid earliest memories date from a few years later. We would play horsey, with me climbing on his back, riding him as he would crawl across the floor. The roles could not be reversed: he was much too large for me then. He was my big brother, the memory of which never fully left either of us; no matter that he

---

flew to NYC to celebrate Channukah with our daughter and grandchildren. A week upon returning to San Diego, Lauren had a paxlovid rebound. This time we waited until the fourth day, after she felt "properly" ill, before restarting her again on paxlovid. (01/12/2024)

barely grew to five feet tall, or never truly went through puberty, and needed to be in a controlled environment, taken care of, his entire life.

After the doctors, the next challenge for my mother was the public education establishment. From kindergarten through high-school, getting Richie into classes where he could learn while receiving additional attention as needed (to handle his other physical needs) was an ever, ongoing battle. What particularly infuriated my mother were the decision makers (the principals, vice-principals, the directors of education, etc.) beseeching special acknowledgment, peacocking for gratitude, whenever Richie was placed in a program. "They're just doing their job", she'd say. "Richie is owed an education like any other child in the district."

12/26/2023

Growing up, we knew we were different. Going to different classes, eventually different schools, seemed ordinary, a given. The difficulty came as I grew. As a child, I was typically at the smaller end of the class (a status that would last until I reached college, where I grew 3 inches and gained 30 pounds, to become average, though still thin). This fact helped delay the inevitable: he no longer being the bigger brother. For him, that was the hardest change to accept.

For me, it was his difference. There was a period growing up when I was embarrassed being seen with him. Visibly different, behaviorally different; it seemed a crap-shoot whether he'd suddenly have an irruption when we might disagree when being the "bigger" brother no longer applied. A sudden yell, followed by an out pore of refusal mixed with tears. In the street, or in a store, or at the mall, going to a movie, it didn't matter where, but particularly at a movie, when the possibility of food came up. All the attention, the stares, the embarrassment. And the shame later of that embarrassment.

I knew as I got older that this was who he was, that he couldn't help it. And so, I learned to ignore the stares. In high school, I'd tell my friends I didn't care what others thought. They thought, I am sure, it was mere bravado, and bravado was surely mixed in, but ultimately it was Rich. He was my gauntlet, my mentor: to never be embarrassed of those you love.

(12/27/2023)

Richie had Prader-Willi syndrome; a genetic disorder first described in the literature in 1956, just three years prior to Rich's birth. He was not diagnosed with the syndrome until 1978, during my first year in college. After I learned of the diagnosis, I immediately headed to the library to learn whatever I could about Prader-Willi. It was my first endeavor pluming original research papers. The relevant journals (this was well before the internet) were housed in the life-sciences building; another first, my going in there. And after familiarizing myself with the library's labyrinth of stacks, and the indexing system used by each journal to classify the work reported each year, I found late at night what I was seeking: a review article on Prader-Willi. I can still recall when first finding photos of other patients with the syndrome: the oval-shaped body; the distinctive eyes. I had never before seen anyone else like Rich and now here was being described the full-laundry list of his health problems. Only some had been apparent at birth. Cognitive disability, short stature, high pain threshold, and what proved to be with Richie the most pressing daily problem: an unrestrained appetite due to the absence of the normal satiation mechanism that resulted in persistent food seeking, often leading, as in his case, to obesity. Over the years, my father had to install locks on our refrigerator doors and to the food pantry, to prevent Rich's forays. These were never full-proof: the challenge of a determined, single-minded adversary. Growing up, my mother told me the behavior was compulsive, uncontrollable; that Rich himself knew it was irrational, afterward; like once after a binge when she found raw bacon missing (after he woke up from a deep sleep following a produced stupor). And finally, in seemingly deadly partnership with these compulsions, one-third of those studied had diabetes. Rich had just been identified to belong to this minority, his blood sugar being found well over 200. Indeed, it was this last puzzle piece (and the diffusion time then prevalent forty-plus years ago of research results on rare genetic disorders) that finally brought us to an expert that deciphered Rich to be Prader-Willi.

For the next few months, Rich was in the hospital, to get his blood-sugar down and to lose weight. By the end of my freshman year, Rich was back home, but my parents knew they had to make more permanent arrangements for him; home was no longer safe. My mother always knew that when they grew old, staying home was not a viable option, and that eventually Rich would need a solution not involving them. Eventually had now come.

My mother learned that New Jersey, our neighboring state (and home to Atlantic Chemical Corporation, the company my father represented as a technical salesman) had recently opened dedicated housing facilities for residents with Prader-Willi syndrome. The progressive nature of the State was two-fold: not only were there living facilities for special needs adults, but Prader-Willi had reached sufficient awareness within the medical community that enough adults were being identified and diagnosed, and that the unique needs of those with the syndrome required a special facility onto itself. Getting admitted, despite coming from New York City, turned out to be easy. The first year though was a financial strain, as it would take that time to establish Rich as a New Jersey resident and thus a ward of the state. Coupled with my college tuition, the hardship was palpable, my father adding long hours in his lab, expanding his secondary consulting income. But in the end, it worked. Rich had a new home. Happy, not a burden, where for the next forty years, he would be looked after, taken care of, by dedicated, caring workers; my parent's final gift to us, my sister and me.

12/26/2023

I never got a chance to speak at Richie's funeral. The plan, my mother had told me, was for him to be buried with my parents at Miramar National Cemetery. It was the plan we knew, my sister and I, and that he, Richie, knew. But when the time came, I found no formal arrangements had been made. Richie, as the disabled son of a veteran, had the right to be buried with his parents at Miramar. We though had to prove that fact: that he was disabled, and the son of our father. This required obtaining a copy of his birth certificate for the latter, and a letter from his doctor for the former. And without proof of a destination, the funeral home in Camden could not release Richie's body and put it onto a plane to San Diego. And as just a sibling, and not his parents, the official bureaucratic friction was ever more alert, ever more resistant. The only fault in the hand-off I could ascribe to my mother. But by the time these intentions were announced, she was much older and had her hands full taking care of my father.

Rich was finally buried two months later. I wasn't at his funeral. This entire effort now may indeed be just a recompense for that absence. At least a little; hopefully more than that.

Nearly a year earlier, we had booked with a group of friends a riverboat cruise for the Tulip Season in the Netherlands. Initially, when Rich died on March 3rd, I thought for sure we had plenty of time before our planned departure. But as the weeks became months, and the official channels remained glacial, I said to Lauren, "What's the point of canceling? We might still be waiting by the time we come back." Sure enough, while in Bruges, over a rich Belgian beer with friends who had traveled down from England, I got the call from the cemetery that Rich's burial had been approved. And of course, they now wanted to move quickly. I put them in touch with my sister, and she with our Rabbi, and Richie was finally buried May 5th. We "attended" over Zoom, but the connection was so poor, the services being held outside near his gravesite, that I never got to speak. No disrespect that: the dead don't care, funerals are for the living, but for the living perhaps it mattered. And so again, this.

Had I spoken, I knew what I would say. That:

"Rich made me better. Without knowing it, without intending it, Rich made me better. Not a path I'd recommend, or prescribe, to anyone, yet still the truth. My parents made me the man I am, but Rich made me better. For that I am grateful. I love him and will miss him. "

Still miss him, as I do my parents. His grave is just one over from the grave my parents share. In the end, the Cemetery had done him/us well.

12/27/2023

Grateful too that he outlasted my mother. For a while it wasn't certain he would; both were declining, he needing a cane, she using a walker: both with congestive heart failure. For some time, I thought he felt like an old, old man. Not that he knew; he'd say "Can you believe I am sixty" (or later, sixty-one, and then sixty-two), "Can you believe it? I look young!" And indeed, his face, his eyes, kept that same look from his baby photos. But he was old, like my grandfather or father near the end, much older than his years. Grateful therefore my mother preceded him. That that wasn't confronted, or hidden from her, like I did with my cousin Bill's passing during her last months as she was slipping away in hospice.

(12/28/2023)

This is my third book. With each book I've had an intended audience; at least one for whom I meant, hoped, it would be read. For the first, it was my daughter, written soon after her wedding. For the second was my grandson (now grandsons). This one is I suppose for Rich. Impossible I know. Not just because he's now gone, but because for the Rich I knew, it wouldn't make sense, this. No, not for him, but for the Rich that never was. The Rich deprived my parents; the Rich that should have been.

12/27/2023

In short, I suppose, it is for me.

I keep coming back to Job. Or perhaps it's more accurate to say, that I keep coming back to Rich, who became Job after my aunt introduced me to the book as a late teen when I first entered college. The injustice. The unshakeable, at times, while growing up, an overwhelming sense of unfairness. What Rich was missing, would never be; what my parents would never see; the cousins my daughter would never have. J'Accuse…! Come, come the whirlwind: speak, chastise, reprimand. Anything! Any voice but my own.

Rich is happy, my father would say. At what cost, I'd think, I'd dispute? Is that enough?

Other times though, talking about other things, my father would tell me with his typical swagger (once a marine always a marine) that when he meets God he'd demand He explain Himself. Pride approaching the sacrilegious I thought, suggested, then; now, not so sure, seeming instead, in retrospect, containing a kernel of just the opposite: more, that is, like a statement of faith.

(02/22/2024)

I saw him after surgery. And the next day. I had feared that he would never wake up, thinking that that was the crucial hurdle. Years earlier other doctors had ruled out bypass surgery, explaining his arteries were too small. But now, with further advances, at one of the country's best cardio facilities, he had made it yet again, I thought: success.

He was most concerned about his meals: not missing breakfast; ordering lunch, dinner, and snacks. He could hardly eat, but knowing the food was there and would be coming, that his routine would be unbroken, was comfort. I turned on the TV and after a while, knowing Philip was waiting downstairs, asked if I could go. Looking at the screen, slowly chewing, he nodded and said yes. We said goodbye. I said I loved him and he replied he loved me, my departing exchange ever since my father became ill; the last words we'd say to each other.

Later that day I received a call that they had to sedate and intubate Rich again; his kidneys had begun to fail. The bypasses were tested: they were all holding; the blood to his heart was flowing. But the shock of the surgery to his system, a system I knew was frail, a system I knew from past stays in the hospital (long nights, emergency vehicle runs) when he visited my mother and us in San Diego, I knew was always precipitously in a delicate balance; to this system, the surgery had proved too much. Two days later Rich was dead.

I had just gotten back to San Diego. I was needed at home; Lauren had an upcoming procedure. I knew there was nothing more I could do for Rich, attached to all the machines; that either he would wake up, or he wouldn't. Perhaps I had already suspected the inevitable: the needs of the living always come first. That very evening of my return, I received a call from his attendant doctor asking me if I wanted any extraordinary procedures done. I said no, no to pain; his body had seen enough, time to give him peace. And as we sat on the couch, Lauren next to me, phone in hand, Rich's heart stopped.

Ronnie

Next in time, next in significance (though not to Lauren, nor to Becky), came Ronnie, my sister-in-law. She was first diagnosed with gallbladder cancer in August 2022. Treatment, for what it was, having hardly changed for over twenty years, began almost immediately. Nefarious, particularly deadly, despite being in an organ regularly excised, gallbladder cancer. The key to surviving cancer, any cancer, is early detection. Lauren has now survived three such bouts. But for gallbladder cancer, being rare, without early warning tests, by the time one first notices it, the discomfort, the cramps, by then it's already spread, metastasized. First stop, the liver; inoperable.

12/28/2023

Lauren and Ronnie talked every day on the phone, usually for an hour, sometimes two. Sometimes it was late when they spoke. Ronnie, living on the East Coast, three time zones ahead of us, initiated those calls. At those times she often had a presentation due tomorrow, and she was taking a break, or procrastinating. She thrived on deadlines: the adrenalin surge. My complete opposite. I'd want plenty of time to step back, do a second revision, then a third. Hated working with/for someone who didn't give me that option, who creates false emergencies: who is the emergency. But that was Ronnie's modus operandi. Lauren always answered, happy to talk: understood what was going on.

She feels the hole, those hours no more. She'll tear up; will do so I suppose for years to come.

Ronnie had a Ph.D. in organizational communications from Michigan State University. She and Philip met in Michigan. He was working in the State's public education system, the field in which he has his Ph.D. The story she'd tell is that they met when she was still a student, working in a government office (East Lansing, the home of MSU, is also the State Capitol). In walked Philip, on his way, as part of his job, to see the department head. He stopped and engaged in small talk with another woman in the office, an older woman, who knew Philip from his regular visits. Somehow the conversation turned to whether he planned on getting married, and he replied yes. And when she asked to whom, he turned and pointed at Ronnie.

Fifty years later, they were still together.

Despite motion sickness, Ronnie loved to travel. Paris and London were regular destinations, their traditional Thanksgiving. They had been to China when it first opened up in the 80s. We went many years later after the Sino-communist version of capitalism had taken off. Japan and Turkey became destinations for us too after

Ronnie had described to Lauren their adventures there. We've now been to Turkey twice, once to Istanbul when Becky did her year abroad in Jordan. Magnificent, steeped in history, the only city that I've seen that could rival Rome, offering two distinctly separate pinnacles of civilization. The second time to Ephesus as part of our cruise of the Greek Isles. Both were before Erdogan. Before the reclaiming of the Hagia Sophia. We'd not go back now. Last summer (2022) we had been to Hungary; a stop on a cruise of the Danube. They, Ronnie and Philip, had loved Budapest; and talked about it before our trip. On the surface, wonderful: grand Budapest; the bridges, the old castle converted to a museum overlooking the Danube, and the magnificent parliament too on the river. And the cuisine! But the history, the history we couldn't ignore. Lauren's uncle (by marriage) was Hungarian and had fled the Nazis, having to seek shelter, disguised, from the prevailing native anti-Semitism: no import from Hitler needed. The history: the tactful embrace mid-century of one murderous regime after another, a history unlike that of Germany (home to the leader of the free world during the Trump years, Angela Merkel) or in Japan, a history having been confronted, expunged, now past. In Hungary still alive, still palpable, in its illiberal democracy. We couldn't shake that history, that present. No, we'll not go back there either; probably should never have even gone at all. I don't know if we'll ever get to Buenos Aires, another one of Ronnie's delights; too much of a shadow cast by October 7th.

For the last fifteen years, Ronnie lived in Philadelphia. After leaving Ann Arbor, they moved to South Orange, New Jersey, then to the Hamptons on Long Island, and lastly Philadelphia, all as Philip pursued opportunities after retiring from Michigan. Whenever we visited them in Philadelphia, Ronnie always made sure to pick up from Carlino's an order of cannoli, my favorite dessert. There are some bakeries in New York City that make cannoli as good as Carlino's, but none better. She'd present them with a big smile, her joy. A treat always.

Ronnie was an Executive consultant and coach, sought by companies, some major, Dow Jones listed. In her prime, she flew all over the country, consulting, presenting at conferences, a sought speaker. When I left physics (jettisoned) and moved to San Diego having landed a job in a high-tech software company specializing in the commercial applications of Artificial Intelligence (back then, in 1996, before the deluge of graduates in the field, companies were willing to train new hires, or at least this company, HNC, was; focusing in their hiring decision on a demonstration that the investment would pay off) she helped me navigate the new world into which I had plunged. The corporate ladder, and the demands of management (both from and as) as I began to succeed and get promoted. Once I coordinated through Ronnie a management training program for the department (Fraud), I was part of. A great asset it was having on one's speed dial, free of charge, an industry expert, an executive consultant.

Now it had become Becky's turn to turn to Ronnie for input. With the turmoil she's had over the summer, her funding at the non-profit having run out (redirected by the donor to other causes); the attempt to rebrand herself and move into another component of the non-profit "business". Outside my expertise, perhaps more than any of us, besides just missing her, she could most use Ronnie now.

Rich was old for many years, his death though sudden at sixty-two. Ronnie died September 14th, one month before her 73rd birthday. It had been the diagnosis, fourteen months earlier that had been sudden, derailing. Not just because being cancer, but this particular cancer: virulent, unrelenting; too rare to have gotten much attention; not rare enough to be irrelevant. Her death we could see coming, the treatment had stopped being effective back in March, when the markers that had been on a steady decrease stopped declining and instead turned abruptly upward. After fourteen months, all the planning for her retirement, the future trips with Philip, the prideful eye on her daughter, recently married, on her plans and life, after fourteen months all that would stop; at seventy-two not young, but not old either.

Over the last few months, it seemed at times that she was in denial. Talking at times about her next trip to London. And later, when it was becoming equally impossible, just to the Whitney in New York City. At times she seemed confused, not remembering discussions had yesterday, or even thirty minutes before. All a result of the treatment. Poison. No such thing as targeted poison, just the hope the cancer, as growing cells, will preferentially absorb it. As will any other fast-growing cells. And apparently, in Ronnie's case, after many months, these included the hippocampus cells in the brain too. Once she told Lauren she had apologized for a rare blow-up months ago, something she never did, that had hurt another, a loved one. She had never apologized. She thought she did, must have intended to do it, imagined doing it, but never actually apologized. And she meant it; both the remembering doing it, and its intent too.

I question how much she was really in denial. Ronnie was too smart. She'd talk about what she wanted for a funeral. About what Philip would do when she was gone. That he would get another dog. They had to put down theirs in June, due to an inoperable growth. A decision that was accelerated after a skirmish with his groomer. Another losing, a speeding up it seemed, so unnecessary.

Philip has a new dog today.

We fancy a summing up, an epiphany. A reconciling, a welcoming. Not this shrinking, this diminishing, this withering away; or at least so it seems from the outside.

The night she died, she whispered to Philip, he tells us, softly repeating, as that's all she had the strength for, "Everything will be OK, everything will be OK". They both went to sleep. He woke up; she did not.

I don't think she was in denial. No, not at all.

Work

The first in time, the least important, but most disruptive; it seems right, after Ronnie, after our relationship, she and I, to talk about Work now.

12/30/2023

A week before Thanksgiving 2022 my partner scheduled a meeting at the San Diego airport. He wanted to discuss "restructuring". I should have known something was amiss. The last few weeks though had been its own crucible. Lauren had been in the hospital for a gastro-bleed. In the initial event, while she was picking up dinner at the local Thai restaurant, she lost a pint of blood. She immediately felt faint. Sitting down, she gave me a call. I rushed over on foot and drove us across town to the hospital. The nearest hospital was within 10 minutes but none of Lauren's doctors were there. All her specialists were at UCSD. We saw the bleeding was stopping, and Lauren was still conscious, so we agreed I'd take her to the UCSD medical center in La Jolla. Arriving because of a bleed, at the emergency room she was seen right away. The bleed we learned was due to liver damage. One of the nurses the first night treated her poorly, dismissively, judging that she was an alcoholic. That was unacceptable and Lauren complained and the nurse was replaced (I had gone home for the night, seeing that she was stable, needing to take care of our dog). Lauren hardly touched alcohol anymore. The liver damage was due to one or more of the medications she had taken over the last thirty years for her Crohn's disease. The pattern being that the effectiveness of any one drug would decay over time, needing to be replaced every handful of years. Eventually, one is left with drugs with little long-term data, with unknown side effects. Like liver damage.

We had to wait two nights for a bed in the hospital before Lauren could be moved out of the emergency unit. In the hospital room, she had a second bleed. The gastroenterologist explained that due to damage, Lauren's liver could not process blood as fast as her healthy heart was pumping it. This resulted in backlog, swelling the veins into the liver. Most of the veins are surrounded by tissue that provides pressure and limits how much the vein can actually expand, but those veins coming off the gastro tract have a natural cavity into which to balloon. And burst. After a few days, they conducted an endoscopy to tie off any more swelling veins. This has now become a recurring procedure every few months. Lauren also takes blood pressure medicine to lower the overall rate of flow into the liver. There are more aggressive, more invasive, measures that can be taken, but as of yet they are not needed. We won't know until they are; there are no manifest symptoms, no forewarning, no otherwise daily impact, until another bleed.

Lauren was suspicious. Years earlier, during our formative stages, the two of us had similarly jettisoned a potential third partner. We had determined he had nothing to contribute: that he wanted to be a manager, while we needed builders. We met at the Los Angeles airport and united we delivered our decision. As I drove down to the San Diego airport, echoes of that earlier meeting replayed in my head.

B. delivered an extensive presentation on the history of the Company: our initial aspirations, market size, and revenue projections. In the early days, I was the engine for development and innovation. All the code was based on my work; indeed, it still is, after though having been refactored by more structured-oriented hires. On one slide B. included a photo of me with true luminaries. I think this was only half flattery, half intended manipulation; beneath laid sincere respect. Reviewing our growth, and our hires, we came up to the present day.

We had floundered. Not only was our revenue a good factor of 10 below our initial forecasts (a fact obvious for a while now), but this past year, for the first time, our revenue had shrunk. Having kept our team lean, everyone would still be well-compensated (at least in comparison to their previous packages before joining us), but the concern was the trend. If the decay persisted, we'd closed shop within 5 years. B. and I would be all right, but the others would be scrambling. B. felt particular loyalty to J. who had left his Wall Street job to join us as a junior partner. Being 10+ years younger than me, and both having married late, he and B. had young children. I always thought this was an advantage, making them hungry. We had met, and worked together at Fair Isaac, on a product launch I was spearheading. Like most startups, I suppose, I thought we were different. A family: the very word used recently to describe the difference by one of our first hires. I had held B.'s firstborn in the hospital the day she was born. Hungry they were: but it was no longer an advantage to me.

B. and J.'s solution to our crisis was cost cutting, to eject me as a partner. They still wanted to keep me on as a paid employee, to pursue new markets, new business opportunities (reliving the early days). But I was to be cut out of the main (faltering) flow. B. argued he knew how to solve the revenue downturn; that the work would be a grind; that he would get lesser-paid hires, perhaps from Mexico or Romania (J. and B.'s native lands, respectively), better suited for the work. Funding this restructuring would be the removal of what they counted as one major overhead: me.

The company was/is an LLC. B. and I, as founding members, were each, according to the documents filed with California, senior co-owners. As we sat talking, my raising objections, asserting my status as owner, I envisioned the possible futures and saw this was a break. Irrevocably, irredeemably, a break. After 15 years, B. and I had come to an end. If I refused, he would take J. and at least a handful of others, the key production team, take all the machines, and go dark. The entire system would keep running, keep investing, only I would be out. It would be disruptive to the team. I could do likewise, but there are some key production elements that B. had in his pocket and that would take time for me to reproduce. Alternatively, I could sue, bringing legal action, but I knew that that would take years, where only the lawyers would make money, would get anything out of it.

B. was on a strict deadline to catch his return flight home. As the meeting concluded and I left the conference room, I looked back and told B. that I loved him like a brother, only that I didn't know which brother from the bible he was. I am not a religious man, but he is, and I am literate enough to turn a good phrase.

I decided to settle, to get bought out. After all the machinations, and revenue projections (based on the past year's decline), we agreed on a not particularly lucrative figure. A payment was made, and the dissolution of the partnership was formally executed to end the calendar year. A complete decoupling would take another half-year or so. For health insurance purposes, I formally stayed on as a company employee until after my birthday in February, so that if we so chose, we could keep California Cobra until I became eligible for Medicare (Lauren would roll on sooner). Then there were the Company tax filings for 2022. The government announced that these could be delayed until October. By pushing them, B. and J. got it done by June. We've not talked since.

Adrift.

I had not thought of retiring. When I did, it was a distant event, sometimes when I was seventy or so, like my father was. Financially I think we're okay, although I hadn't been planning on living yet off of our savings, potentially (hopefully) for decades. And with Becky, and her two boys, I hadn't achieved all my financial goals. Not that they should need it. She, they, have their own lives. In principle not my role, not my responsibility, not anymore. But one can't, one doesn't stop. The concern, the worry, the planning for the unknown; not fully, to be honest, without cause.

What next then?

This disruption, this severing. This contraction. A loss of comradery. Of trust. The least important of this year, this loss. Yet seemingly, at times that is, the most tangible, the most palpable, this non-time consuming.

12/31/2023

Miriam

Miriam died on October 5, a little over a year after being diagnosed with bowel cancer. Over the course of her treatment the mass in her abdomen, the mass giving her pain, had shrunk, nearly to nonexistence, no longer even a discomfort. But they couldn't keep the cancer from spreading, first to her spine, a location she was told they hoped to simply contain, and then lastly, last summer, to her brain. The neurologist in the hospital, speaking out of turn, told her she had two months to live. That upset Miriam to no end. Her oncologist, never so blunt, was not so definitive. Lauren, with so much experience in these matters, repeated what her oncologist told all his patients: that there's not an expiration date stamped on your forehead. In the end, though, the neurologist was right, nearly to the day.

Growing up we weren't very close. She was the second in the line of cousins, each in the succession separated by one year. My mother and her sisters' offspring. Two more, Daniel and Alyta, would come later, breaking the pattern. I was the last in the chain, four years younger than Miriam. It wasn't until we were older that that gap wasn't decisive.

Two years earlier she had gone to Bill's funeral. Glioblastoma. Fourteen months after diagnosis; the expected expectancy, right on track. I last saw him just after he was diagnosed, in February 2020. He said he'd like to drive across the country, saying he never had. In my head I planned how we could do it, the two of us. His last adventure, my last time with him. Never happened: Covid. He died on the day I got my first injection, March 18, 2021. Never got to Bill's funeral. With Lauren being immune compromised, I wouldn't risk travel until I was fully vaccinated. But Miriam would, did. She had to say goodbye. We talked about the funeral. I didn't recognize over Zoom, in its emphasis on the deathbed conversion (done I suspected at least as much for his sister as for himself, as though the Divine, if that is the one listening, would care, would make it the fulcrum, this clamor, this pretense) the Bill I knew. Miriam said the talk the night before was better. The reminiscing, the laughter as was Bill's way. As was Miriam's. She had to go. I could not. Over lunch in New York City, after we could travel, Lauren, Miriam and I talked and laughed some more.

Even to her dying gasp her facial features were striking; I always thought of Elizabeth Taylor when I saw her. She was married and divorced once. I didn't realize it at the time, but I think he was abusive. Not physically (or so I know), but emotionally, and mentally, isolating her from her friends, and her community. No kids, probably for the better. Miriam always had a troubled relationship with her mother. That had toned down over the years. When Miriam was sick, they spoke every day. Her mother was the target, but I think much actually originated with her father, Milton. Her friend Jessicka, who heroically cared for Miriam the last month, confided that as a woman she always felt in competition with her when men were around. Competition for their attention, for their affirmation. Strange. Jessicka was at least fifteen years younger than Miriam. I think that was Milton.

He's been dead twenty years now, having died from multiple myeloma, a painful type of cancer that targets the bones. Treatment has not greatly improved that much since then: my friend Aron died two years ago of the same.[3] He was just 62. Milton was luckier; he got to know his grandson Natan, the son of David. David died 37 years ago from cancer too, just after Natan was born. A bad history; looks to course through the Nelson line. My aunt is 91: there's a price to pay for longevity. Daniel is 55; he knows to aggressively monitor his health. He has Solange to prod him.

Miriam had no one, no one that is, she'd listen to. Solange says it was almost a full year after the first indications, the first discomforts in the belly, before Miriam got herself examined. I hadn't learned that until the end when Miriam lay unconscious on her deathbed. No wonder this past year she'd get so upset. To the end she fought, in tears, she'd state she didn't want to die. Some mistakes, particularly when we're young, we learn from, are growth opportunities. Others we don't survive. As a young man, I got angry, anger being the privilege of the young, at my uncle Victor when he died from diabetes, believing the disease could have been, should have been, treated better. Perhaps so, but in the end, he didn't want to die either, didn't want to leave his wife, his children, his grandchildren. No one

---

[3] Perhaps that's what killed Dimpy too. By the time her cancer was detected it was already in stage 4. I never learned what type of cancer it was; seems like the doctors didn't even know. But her bones became fragile, suffering a shattered hip on an examination table, when the physician had pressed too hard. She lasted less than a year. (02/26/24)

regretted more the outcome. Miriam too.

After it was over, after we saw Miriam breathe her last (I had stayed, didn't want her, didn't want Daniel to be alone (Solange having had to go home to take care of their son), not a time to be alone, a time to be with family, with loved ones), I told Daniel on a walk, that in the end its because we've loved that we feel this sorrow; that were we alone we'd have no loss. "I am grateful." I said, "For the love, for not being alone. And hence, in its own way, no matter how unfair, and unfair it surely is, I can, however oddly it is to say, be grateful, grateful for what makes this a loss."

"An interesting way to look at it," he said.

01/01/2024

2
ELEGY

Back to Job, to Rich; always. Less the what (departures, the inverse of birth, that miracle, unbegrudged), than the how and when. Those injustices: the unresolved, unrelenting. But now with a twist: the good (the great) doing bad. Prototypically, two Germans; contemporaries, though without being known interlocutors, at opposite ends of accomplishment, indeed perhaps even adversaries, philosophically. Their focus here, now, reflections, no more, of my own preoccupations, obsessions, over time, over the years; no other defense proffered.

01/02/2024

Heisenberg

Clearing nearly one billion dollars worldwide, the movie *Oppenheimer* was the third highest-grossing film last year. Telling the tale of the "father of the atomic bomb", like most of my physicist friends, and Lauren too who visited with me Los Alamos while I spent a couple of weeks at the lab as a postdoc, I found the movie well done, well-acted, and a bit dull. Since freshman year when I decided to study physics over forty years ago and read Ruth Spier's translation of Heinar Kipphardt's 1968 play *In the Matter of J. Robert Oppenheimer*, and then numerous other accounts about the lab, the technical details, the decision to drop the bomb and the ensuing debate of the morality of that decision, the shadow it cast on the community, there was little new for this audience. Little that is other than the story of Lewis Strauss, wonderfully portrayed by Robert Downey Jr., the diabolical bureaucrat most responsible for the 1954 hearing of the Atomic Energy Commission that revoked Oppenheimer's security clearance. Beneath the Olympus, the history-changing events, the becoming "Death, the destroyer of Worlds", and of who can/should yield such power, a squalid tale of intrigue, of revenge, nothing more. What I did not realize, what I had forgotten in the movie theatre and what was only refreshed afterward, was that the successful development of the hydrogen bomb, the development Oppenheimer had opposed and fought against, was already over 16 months past; "Ivy Mike", 10 megatonnes of TNT yielding device, had been detonated on November 1, 1952; the 15 megatonnes of TNT "Castle Bravo" detonation, the first and largest of the series of tests on Bikini Atoll, was just conducted on March 1, 1954, a month prior to the hearings. Strauss and Teller were clearing house.

Strauss organized/called the AEC hearing. Edward Teller, the "father of the hydrogen bomb" testified "I thoroughly disagreed with him in numerous issues and his actions frankly appeared to me confused and complicated. To this extent, I feel that I would like to see the vital interests of this country in hands which I understand better, and therefore trust more. In this very limited sense, I would like to express a feeling that I would feel personally more secure if public matters would rest in other hands." And "if it is a question of wisdom or judgment, as demonstrated by actions since 1945, then I would say one would be wiser not to grant clearance."[4]

Two months later, Joseph Welch would publicly shame Joe McCarthy. As shown in the movie, Strauss's eclipse came five years later, when he failed to get Senate approval to become Eisenhower's Secretary of Commerce. The revelation of his handling of Oppenheimer was either a defining factor (as told by the movie) or an excuse, a political cover of other behind-the-scene machinations. Oppenheimer's security clearance was never reinstated.[5] And Edward Teller, "the father of the hydrogen bomb", a divisive, long controversial figure, although ostracized by some in the community for his role with Oppenheimer, was never formally impacted, retaining his leading advisory role, becoming in 1958 the first Director of the newly formed Lawrence Livermore National Lab., which he co-founded with Ernst Lawrence and with which he remained affiliated as Director Emeritus until his death in 2003.

Caught in the same maelstrom as Oppenheimer, the

---

[4] U.S. Department of Energy OpenNet, J. Robert Oppenheimer Personnel Hearings Transcripts, Vol XIII;
https://www.osti.gov/includes/opennet/includes/Oppenheimer%20hearings/Vol%20XIII%20Oppenheimer.pdf

[5] 78 years later the DOE would vacate the decision and conclusions reached by their parent organization, the AEC.

https://discover.lanl.gov/publications/national-security-science/2023-summer/in-the-matter-of-j-robert-oppenheimer/

story of Werner Heisenberg is of a different sort.

This is an elegy. Heisenberg was a great man. Founder of the matrix formulation of quantum mechanics at the age of twenty-five in 1926, he enunciated the eponymous Uncertainty Principle a year later, the key to understanding all atomic (and sub-atomic) phenomena. He recounts that he was inspired by a conversation he had with Einstein[6], who would famously later renounce ("God does not play dice") the inherent underlying indeterminability expressed by the Uncertainty Principle. A beloved member of the Copenhagen school, he was a close sounding board of the school's founder Niels Bohr (Nobel Prize in Physics, 1922), the author years earlier of the "Bohr atom". Bohr and Einstein would famously duel over the implications of Heisenberg's discoveries.[7] Wolfgang Pauli, of the

---

[6] In Chapter 3 of his memoir *Physics and Beyond Encounters and Conversations* (Harper Torch Books, 1971) Heisenberg relates a memorable conversation he had had with Einstein in 1926 in Berlin on the nature of observables. Einstein explained "Perhaps I did use this kind of reasoning, but it is nonsense all the same. Perhaps I could put it more diplomatically by saying that it may be heuristically useful to keep in mind what one has actually observed. But on principle, it is quite wrong to try founding a theory on observable magnitudes alone. In reality the very opposite happens. It is the theory which decides what we can observe." Heisenberg relates in Chapter 4 that it was recalling this conversation in 1927 that triggered his formulation of the Uncertainty Principle.

[7] It is unclear how thoroughly Heisenberg himself understood the significance of his discoveries, repeatedly (*The Physical Principles of the Quantum Theory*, (Dover Publications, 1949), Introduction, pg 3; *Physics and Philosophy: The Revolution in Modern Science,* (Harper Torchbooks,1962), Chapter III, pg. 47) describing the Uncertainty Principle as a consequence of the measuring process. While true in detail it misses the main point: that the uncertainty is an inherent part of nature *prior* to any human observation.

Pauli Exclusion Principle, was a good friend who initially was his guide to the world of research physics[8], and later a student of his work; Max Born, one of his professors while he pursued his Ph.D. in 1923, would too become his student, reinterpreting his (and Schrodinger's) discoveries to cement our understanding that the predictions of quantum mechanics are to be understood as probabilities. Heisenberg was awarded the Nobel Prize in Physics in 1932; Pauli in 1945; Born in 1954. Other than Einstein, Heisenberg was Germany's greatest theoretical physicist of the 20th century. And by the beginning of World War II, the greatest physicist remaining in Nazi Germany.

01/06/2024

In September 1941 Heisenberg visited Bohr in Nazi-controlled Copenhagen (Germany conquered Denmark

---

Nuclear decay (including fission) is a prime example of quantum tunneling, a process forbidden in classical physics made possible by the Uncertainty Principle and one that Heisenberg was well familiar with. In current literature (work developed well after Heisenberg's death) quantum tunneling is a key aspect of modern cosmology ala Superstring theory and the prediction of multiple universes. Recently quantum tunneling has been suggested to be the underlying cause of genetic mutations, the driver of biological evolution. See the review of work at the University of Surrey: https://www.sciencedaily.com/releases/2022/05/220505085605.htm. None of these phenomena involve the epistemological consideration of the impact of the observer on the observed, a consideration known by physicists since at least Galileo. For Galileo's struggles with his telescope, see Paul Feyerabend, *Against Method* 4th edition, Verso Books (New York, 1975).

[8] See Chapter 2 of *Physics and Beyond*. By the time they met, Pauli, nearly 2 year's Heisenberg's elder, had already written a review article on General Relativity and was now extolling the unsolved problems in atomic physics.

in the Spring of 1940). Three years earlier (December 1938), Otto Hahn and Lise Meitner had discovered nuclear fission in Uranium. By February 1939 physicists throughout the world were discussing the possibility of an atomic bomb. In his trip to Bohr, Heisenberg had with him nuclear astrophysicist Carl von Weizsäcker, his protégé and son of SS member Ernst von Weizsäcker, State Secretary at the Foreign Office, the second highest official in the German Foreign Office after Foreign Minister Joachim von Ribbentrop. Carl von Weizsäcker was explicitly mentioned in the Einstein-Szilard letter of August 2, 1939, to Franklin Delano Roosevelt that warned of the potential of Uranium to produce an atomic bomb and urged FDR to launch a nuclear weapons program.[9] FDR's actions in response led to the birth of the Manhattan Project.

Heisenberg and Bohr began their conversation in Bohr's office. Fearing that the office was bugged by the Gestapo, they moved their talk outside, taking one of their long-established strolls in Bohr's gardens. When Bohr escaped Denmark in 1943 and joined the Manhattan Project in Britain and then the United States, he confirmed everyone's worst fears: that Heisenberg and Weizsäcker were working on an atomic bomb. I first learned of this history from Phil Siemens, who gave me my first postdoc. Phil had been a student of Hans Bethe at Cornell University, starting, ever so propitiously as he

---

[9]https://en.wikipedia.org/wiki/Einstein%E2%80%93Szilard_letter

relates it, his thesis with Bethe just prior to Bethe's winning of the Nobel Prize in 1967. Bethe had been at Los Alamos when Bohr visited and relayed his intelligence regarding the Nazi nuclear program. It was the conversation with Heisenberg in 1941 that convinced Bohr of the urgency of the Allies' work.

After the war, Heisenberg and Bohr's accounts of that conversation critically differ. In his 1973 book/memoir, *Physics and Beyond: Encounters and Conversations*, Heisenberg writes:[10]

"In the autumn of 1941, when we thought we had a fairly clear picture of the technical possibilities, we asked the German Embassy in Copenhagen to arrange a public lecture for me there. I think I arrived in Denmark in October 1941, and when I visited Niels in his home in Carlsberg, I did not broach the dangerous subject until we took our evening walk. Since I had reason to think that Niels was being watched by German agents, I spoke with the utmost circumspection. I hinted that it was now possible in principle to build atomic bombs, but that a tremendous technological effort was needed, and that physicists ought perhaps to ask themselves whether they should work in that field at all. Unfortunately, as soon as I mentioned the mere possibility of making atom bombs, Niels became so horrified that he failed to take in the most important part of my report, namely, that an

---

[10] Chapter 15, page 182; *Physics and Beyond*.

enormous technical effort was needed. Now this, to me, was so important precisely because it gave physicists the possibility of deciding whether or not the construction of atom bombs should be attempted. They could either advise their governments that atom bombs would come too late for use in the present war, and that work on them therefore detracted from the war effort, or else contend that, with the utmost exertions, it might just be possible to bring them into the conflict. Both views could be put forth with equal conviction, and, in fact, during the war, it turned out that even in America, where conditions were incomparably more favorable for the attempt than in Germany, the atom bomb was not made ready before V.E. Day."

This choice was the account held by Heisenberg and Weizsäcker since their capture by the Allies in May 1945 and subsequent stay at Farm Hall, England from July 3, 1945—January 6, 1946. Max von Laue, the 1914 Nobel Prize winner in Physics, and another detainee at Farm Hall labeled this account the Farm Hall "Lesart", version of events.[11]

After the announcement on August 6th of the atomic bomb being dropped on Japan, the following conversation at Farm Hall was (secretly?) recorded:

---

[11] In letters to Paul Rosbaud, found in Appendix 2 of Jeremy Bernstein's *Hitler's Uranium Club: The Secret Farm Hall Recordings* (Copernicus Press, 2001).

Heisenberg: We wouldn't have had the moral courage to recommend to the Government in the spring of 1942 that they should employ 120,000 men just for building the thing up.

Weizsäcker: I believe the reason we didn't do it was because all the physicists didn't want to do it on principle. If we had all wanted Germany to win the war, we would have succeeded.

On the next day, August 7th, Weizsäcker would summarize in conversation with Von Laue:

Weizsäcker: History will record that the Americans and English made a bomb, and that at the same time the Germans, under the Hitler regime, produced a workable engine. In other words, the peaceful development of the uranium engine was made in Germany under the Hitler regime, whereas the Americans and the English developed this ghastly weapon of war.

Returning to the Copenhagen meeting of 1941, Bohr always maintained that there was no confusion on his part, and in 1954, after reading Heisenberg's account of that 1941 meeting in a letter by Heisenberg to Robert Jungk, drafted, never sent, but saved, the following in an intended letter dated March 21, 1954:[12]

"However, what I am thinking of in particular is the conversation we had in my office at the Institute, during which, because of the subject you raised, I carefully fixed in my mind every word that was uttered. It had to make a very strong impression on me that at the very outset you stated that you felt certain that the war, if it lasted sufficiently long, would be decided with atomic weapons. I had at that time no knowledge at all of the preparations that were underway in England and America. You added, when I perhaps looked doubtful, that I had to understand that in recent years you had occupied yourself almost exclusively with this question and did not doubt that it could be done. It is therefore quite incomprehensible to me that you should think that you hinted to me that the German physicists would do all they could to prevent such an application of atomic science. During the conversation, which was only very brief, I was naturally very cautious but nevertheless thought a lot about its content, and my alarm was not lessened by hearing from the others at the Institute that Weizsäcker had stated how fortunate it would be for the position of science in Germany after the victory that you could help so significantly towards this end."

I've always found Bohr's version more plausible.

[12] William Sweet, The Bohr Letters No more uncertainty, Bulletin of the Atomic Scientists May/June 2002.
https://journals.sagepub.com/doi/pdf/10.2968/058003007

Heisenberg himself states that they went for a stroll to avoid being monitored. It would be at this time, while recreating those productive walks they had had nearly twenty years earlier, to speak plainly, directly. The responsibility to eliminate any confusion was clearly Heisenberg's. To conclude that he failed seems implausible.

The recordings made by the British at Farm Hall were released to the public in 1992. Having been classified, it is correct to say that they had been "secret". Whether they were in fact secret recordings, i.e., unknown to being made at the time by the detainees at Farm Hall, is generally assumed.[13] I am suspicious.

Soon after their arrival at Farm Hall, Heisenberg had the following (recorded) conversation with Kurt Diebner on July 6th "in presence of a number of their colleagues":

Diebner: I wonder whether there are microphones installed here?

Heisenberg: Microphones installed? (laughing) Oh no, they're not as cut as all that. I don't think they know the real Gestapo methods; they're a bit old fashioned in

---

[13] For a discussion of the tapes, their limitations, and the contrasting interpretations of their meaning, see Ryan Dahn, "The Farm Hall Transcripts: The Smoking Gun that Wasn't", Ber. Wissenschaftsgesch. 45 (2022): 202 – 218. https://onlinelibrary.wiley.com/doi/abs/10.1002/bewi.20210 0033. The released transcripts can be found online at https://discovery.nationalarchives.gov.uk/details/r/C4414534 .

that respect.

Was this assessment by Heisenberg sincere or was it guile? He had already been held hostage by the Allies for over ten weeks. Having lived under the Nazis for the last thirteen years, including an incidence of suspicion in 1937 we'll discuss later, and as we saw with his conversation with Bohr in 1941, he was well experienced with the needed cautions of living while monitored. The Farm Hall transcripts are simply that, transcripts of recorded conversations. We have no idea of the non-verbal communication that took place. Heisenberg could very well of placed his fingers over his lips as he verbally dismissed Diebner's concerns. And even if his reply on July 6th was his sincere first impression, the possibility of being secretly monitored, and recorded, would have surely remained and have been reconsidered. Heisenberg and the nine other detainees at Farm Hall knew they were being held for a reason: their involvement in their so-called "Uranium Club", the Nazi nuclear program. They recognized the inherent instability of the alliance with the Soviet Union; and their significance as potential assets/targets for recruitment by "Russia".[14] They knew that what they knew was valuable. Without crossing over into being viewed as a threat, they sought to best position themselves for the peace that would ensue. All the conversations should be read under this cloud.

---

[14] At Farm Hall, the detainees used Russia or Stalin, to refer to the Soviet Union.

In an interview many years later, Teller argued that Bohr did Heisenberg a disservice.[15] That based on the Farm Hall transcripts it was clear to him (Teller) that Heisenberg had not thought much about fission, as he repeated an error that he himself had made when first estimating the critical mass of Uranium 235 required to make a bomb. [16]

Heisenberg: If I have pure 235 each neutron will immediately beget two children and then there might be a chain reaction which goes very quickly. Then you can reckon as follows. One neutron always makes two others in pure 235. That is to say that in order to make 10^25 neutrons I need 80 reactions one after the other. Therefore I need 80 collisions and the mean free path is about 6 centimetres. In order to make 80 collisions, I would have a lump of radius of about 54 centimetres and that would be about a ton.

It is notable that earlier that day Hahn had asked Heisenberg:[17]

---

[15] https://www.webofstories.com/play/edward.teller/34

[16] In conversation with Hahn on August 6th.

[17] In an otherwise entrancing tale, it is on this point that I find the 2002 BBC film Copenhagen, of Michael Frayn's play of the same name, to falter. Too much emphasis is made at the end of Heisenberg's initial error of the critical mass, as though that was decisive for Germany not pursuing the bomb. Heisenberg quickly corrected that error, if indeed it ever was an error: I've already stated my caveat regarding all of the recorded Farm Hall conversations. More salient is Heisenberg's already quoted, correct assessment (vis a vis the Manhattan project) of the scale of the effort required.

Hahn: But tell me why you used to tell me that one needed 50kg of 235 in order to do anything. Now you say one needs two tons.

This is notable as the correct critical mass is in fact just slightly more than 50kg.

The next day (August 12th) when the weight of the bomb is reported in the newspapers, Heisenberg provides a much more accurate assessment:

Heisenberg: This has worried me considerably and therefore this evening I have done a few calculations and have seen that it is more probable than we had thought on account of the substantial multiplication factors which one can have with fast neutrons. We have always calculated with a multiplication factor of 1.1 because we had found this in practice with uranium. If they have a multiplication factor of 3 or 5 then naturally it is a different matter. We said we need about 80 links in the chain reaction; now the mean free path is 4 cms therefore we must have 80 long divisions (so was the rough estimate) and would then come to about a ton. This calculation is right if the multiplication factor is 1.1 because even then we use nearly every neutron which escapes for multiplication. If on the other hand, the multiplication factor is 3, things are quite different. Then I can say, if the whole thing is only as big as the mean free path, then one neutron which walks around therein once meets another and makes three neutrons, one will already come back, the other two can go off; the one that comes back will for certain make another three. In practice therefore I need only the mean free path for the thing to work.

A week later, on August 14th, Heisenberg gave an extended technical lecture discussing the key parameters for understanding the critical mass required. It is possible that the interest reflected sincere curiosity on the part of the participants. Equally likely was a perceived need to demonstrate their continued value after the war, with the underlying threat to the West implied if they were to be lost to Russia. After a back-and-forth between Heisenberg and the others, they arrive at a critical radius between 6.2 and 13.7cm. The correct size is 8.7cm. They also go on to discuss the possible construction of the bomb, on how to merge two subcritical masses of Uranium into one critical mass at detonation. Heisenberg mentions a gun barrel, very close to the bullet design used in Little Boy, the bomb dropped on Hiroshima.

There is a big difference between white boarding a design and making it work. The Manhattan Project would ultimately swell to over 100,000 people across multiple sites in the United States. Heisenberg's scale of the effort was correct. And that it would be very vulnerable to disruption by Allies attack, as they indeed found for their much smaller program pursuing a nuclear reactor (an "engine"). Whether Teller is right that the conversations at Farm Hall indicate that the Germans never seriously pursued a bomb is mostly irrelevant. Minimally, the transcripts demonstrate that with a little effort, the Germans, and Heisenberg in particular, would unlock the key elements needed. It is striking how he was asked and led all of the technical discussions. In 1941 Bohr learned that Heisenberg was working on Hitler's nuclear program. He was right to be concerned.

Heisenberg was no anti-Semite. He fought the "German Physics" push in the 1930s, led by Nobel Prize winners Philip Lenard and Johannes Stark, to stop teaching the work by physicists of Jewish origin. The target was mostly Einstein. Heisenberg not only personally benefitted, as we've seen, from his talks with Einstein, he knew such efforts were not only nonsense but ultimately would be crippling to German science if successful. His resistance however led to being ominously, and publicly attacked by the SS for his sympathies in the summer of 1937. His status would not be resolved until a year later by Himmler himself who recognized Heisenberg's importance to the Reich but warned him to separate the professional from the personal lives of scientists.[18]

Before the war started, Heisenberg had multiple opportunities to emigrate. In his memoirs, Heisenberg relates the last efforts to convince him to leave, led by Enrico Fermi during his visit to Chicago in the summer of

---

[18] See https://en.wikipedia.org/wiki/Werner_Heisenberg and citations therein.

1939.[19] Heisenberg chose to stay. By his own account, he was looking towards the future, to Germany after Hitler. Even if we accept this reasoning and that in practice that he steered the Nazis away from developing a bomb, we must confront the facts that:

1) The argument against building a bomb was "correct" on purely practical grounds; when it was thought the war would be over quickly, the Nazis would not dedicate the resources required; when the situation turned, they could not. None of this became clear to the Allies until after the war.

2) That Heisenberg never acknowledged the role he played, the shadow he cast, on the Allies bomb effort. As much as the threat Hitler cast, it was the knowledge that Heisenberg was working on Uranium that convinced the community of physicists in the States, native-born (like Oppenheimer and Lawrence) and the vast group of immigrants fleeing the Nazis (like Szilard, Fermi, Bethe, and Teller), to join the Manhattan Project. Had I been alive and had I been asked I certainly would have done so too.

From all accounts, Heisenberg was a religious man, a family man: a good man. But when the whirlwind spoke, the burden of greatness, it was Oppenheimer and not Heisenberg whose integrity remained intact.

---

[19] In chapter 14 of *Physics and Beyond*. While Heisenberg's efforts on an engine during the war remained unfulfilled, Fermi would go on to build the world's first nuclear reactor in 1942. This became the prototype for the Hartford breeder reactors used to generate the plutonium used in Fat Man, the bomb dropped on Nagasaki.

Heidegger

Heidegger was an anti-Semite. That word has taken on an added poignancy since October 7th. The eruption of anti-Semitism across the West[20] has been, beyond appalling, beyond frightening: disorienting. Even before the invasion of Gaza by Israel on October 27th in response to the genocidal slaughter of October 7th, the ADL reported a spike in hate crimes in the United States in the period Oct. 7--23.[21] Similar increases were reported in London[22] and Paris[23]. I stress that this spike occurred immediately after October 7th, before Israel's military response. They were celebrating the slaughter. Shir, Natan's wife, told me she feels safer today in Israel than in Sweden, where they've been living for a year. Anti-Semitism: a dying anachronism, I'd have thought. No more than racism has been after Obama's election.

Hamas's intentions are unambiguously genocidal: the murderous removal of Jews from Israel. If the atrocities of October 7th are not sufficient as proof,

---

[20] Putin has restored the relevance of that term, although geographically it now begins much further East, along the Donbas on the Ukraine-Russian border.

[21] https://www.adl.org/resources/press-release/adl-records-dramatic-increase-us-antisemitic-incidents-following-oct-7

[22] https://www.reuters.com/world/uk/antisemitic-islamophobic-offences-soar-london-after-israel-attacks-2023-10-20/

[23] https://www.reuters.com/world/europe/macron-address-nation-amid-rise-antisemitic-acts-france-2023-10-12/

Hamas' commitment to the open-ended repetition[24] of the slaughter renders their phrase "from the river to the sea" unambiguous. Anyone in a position of power pretending otherwise, is, at best, failing to meet their responsibilities.[25] At worst, it is something much more malevolent. Another consequence: clarity.

Anti-Zionism is today anti-Semitism. As has "colonialism" become another mask for anti-Semitism. The Palestinian death count in Gaza has been tragic, yet a tragedy that is part of Hamas' strategy. An enduring cease-fire is for them, victory. A return to October 6th. Hence the reason to endanger schools, and hospitals; the reason to NOT allow civilian access to their vast network of tunnels, to NOT provide them with safe shelter. The greater the death toll, the greater the outcry abroad. Not cowardice, hiding behind civilians: something much more sinister.

That does not mean Israel cannot be criticized. Netanyahu's time has passed, and his pretense as a strongman of security exploded. Chamberlain knew when to leave. Netanyahu has not. Beyond his opposition to a two-state solution, beyond his naivety supporting Qatar's funding of Hamas as late as September 2023[26], the security failure on October 7th is

---

[24] https://www.jpost.com/arab-israeli-conflict/article-771199

[25] https://www.nbcnews.com/politics/congress/rep-rashida-tlaib-faces-criticism-democrats-palestinian-remarks-rcna123735

[26] https://www.nytimes.com/2023/12/10/world/middleeast/israel-qatar-money-prop-up-hamas.html

his. That fact coupled with an inherent desire to redeem himself, casts a shadow over all he now does. Particularly regarding the anticipated duration of the war that simultaneously delays his public reckoning by maintaining his formal leadership. It might be that all the military decisions are right, driven by the IDF, but Netanyahu undermines their credibility. Internally Israel might, despite the overwhelming lack of support[27] for Netanyahu, rationalize his staying in place until the war's conclusion, but it is wrong. For defining the peace, the future governance of Gaza, the reshaping/replacing the moribund PLO in the West Bank, Israel requires leadership that can, with the support of the United States, reengage with her neighbors, the Iran leery, Arab world. A noncredible Netanyahu can no longer be the face of Israel.

01/10/2024

Heidegger's anti-Semitism was of a different sort than that of the jihad Hamas or of the racial biologism of his Nazi brethren. Nor, significantly, did he ever advocate physical extermination, ala the Final Solution or "from the river to the sea". Heidegger's anti-Semitism was more abstract, what Donatella Di Cesare[28] has called a "metaphysical" anti-Semitism. One though that aligned Jews with most of the purported evils of the

---

[27] https://www.reuters.com/world/middle-east/only-15-israelis-want-netanyahu-keep-job-after-gaza-war-poll-finds-2024-01-02/

[28] Donatella Di Cesare, *Heidegger and the Jews: The Black Notebooks*, Polity (Cambridge, 2018).

modern world. One that saw Jewish culture as an enemy of German greatness. One that envisioned a future cleansed of the influences of that culture. In other words, one whose utopia was a future without Jews.

This is an elegy. Heidegger was a great man. He is arguably the most influential philosopher of the 20th century. His magnus opus *Being and Time*, published in 1927, influenced multiple generations, and multiple movements of Continental thought. His discussion of anxiety, Being-toward-death, and authenticity strongly shaped the direction of French Existentialism. Both Sartre and de Beauvoir acknowledge Heidegger's influence in their respective magnus opuses, *Being and Nothingness*[29] and *The Second Sex*[30]. Dasein ("being there", "being in the world"), Heidegger's term for thinking, questioning man, is inextricably tied to Being; Heidegger's nebulous, quasi-mystic term of the prime importance, a forgotten beginning, a presence evoked repeatedly in his later works, in their turn away from the "humanistic" focus on Dasein of *Being and Time*, that in

---

[29] Jean-Paul Sartre, *Being and Nothingness,* translated by Hazel E. Barnes (Citadel Press, New York, 1956). While there are scattered references throughout, particularly in Part I, see specifically the detailed discussion in Part III on Heidegger in the section "The Existence of Others". George Steiner's assessment is not entirely off, "The existentialism of Jean-Paul Sartre is, explicitly, a version and variant of the idiom and propositions of *Sein und Zeit*." *Martin Heidegger* (The University of Chicago Press, Chicago, 1978).

[30] Simone de Beauvoir, *The Second Sex,* first complete and unabridged edition in English, translated by Constance Borde and Shelia Malovay-Chevallier (First Vintage Books, 2011), see index therein for references to Heidegger.

distinctly ambiguous, oracular terms, are as though by a prophet announcing his cold, dark, hidden God. In *Of Spirit*[31], Derrida equates deconstruction with Heidegger's program of "destruktion" of western metaphysics called for in *Being and Time*. A "destruktion" that would ultimately be extended to *Being and Time* itself.[32]

01/12/2024

Heidegger was a member of the Nazi Party from 1933-1945. He joined two weeks after being elected rector of the University of Freiburg on April 22. Three months earlier (January 30, 1933) Hitler had been appointed Chancellor by President von Hindenburg. Heidegger's conversion was a major victory at the time for the Nazis, providing a veneer of legitimization for the new regime. Edmund Husserl, Heidegger's once mentor, and early champion, to whom Heidegger dedicated *Being and Time*, and who would assure Heidegger's appointment as chair of philosophy at Freiburg upon his own retirement from the position in 1928, would write in a letter to Dietrich Mahnke, on May 4, 1933[33], "The perfect conclusion to this supposed bosom friendship of

---

[31] Jacques Derrida *Of spirit: Heidegger and the question*, translated by Geoffrey Bennington and Rachel Bowlby (The University of Chicago Press, 1987).

[32] Philippe Lacoue-Labarthe, *Heidegger, Art and Politics*, translated by Chris Turner (Basil Blackwell, 1990).

[33] From *Becoming Heidegger*, Theordore Kisiel and Thomas Sheehan (Northwestern University Press 2007), p. 413.

two philosophers was his very public, very theatrical entrance into the Nazi Party on May 1." Husserl notably continued:

"Prior to that there was his self-initiated break in relations with me – in fact, soon after his appointment at Freiburg – and, over the last few years, his anti-Semitism, which he came to express with increasing vigor – even against the coterie of his most enthusiastic students, as well as around the department."

Heidegger stepped down as rector in April 1934. He had apparently aspired to become the Party's intellectual leader, aspirations thwarted by the cruder, more virulent racism of his competition within the Party, notably Alfred Rosenberg.[34] Rosenberg was a longtime member of Hitler's inner circle and was the author of the 1930 screed *The Myth of the Twentieth Century,* an encapsulation of Nazi hate, myth, and advocation of violence to obtain racial purification. Rosenberg was appointed head of cultural policy and surveillance of the Party on January 27, 1934. Heidegger's retreat was no

---

[34] See his Letter to the Rector of Freiburg University of November 4 1945, an undoubtedly self-serving account, where Heidegger writes "During the few days of Christmas vacation I realized that it was a mistake to believe that, from the basic spiritual position that was the result of my long years of philosophical work, I could immediately influence the transformation of the bases—spiritual or non-spiritual—of the National Socialist movement." Previously he mentioned his "opposition to [Alfred] Rosenberg's conception, according to which, conversely, spirit and the world of spirit are merely an "expression" and emanation of racial facts and of the physical constitution of man." Chapter 3, Richard Wolin *The Heidegger Controversy* (The MIT Press, 1993).

coincidence; he would be suspected, his lectures monitored, by Nazi purists for the remaining years of the regime.

During his year as rector, his public support as Hitler consolidated power was however genuine and indeed enthusiastic. He fully supported the recasting of the University as a vehicle of State power, denigrating academic freedom, and extolling Labor Service (work camps) to both physically and spiritually mold the new generation. In support of the November plebiscite to leave the League of Nations, Heidegger on multiple occasions addressed the University along the lines spoken on November 3rd, "The Fuhrer alone is the present and future German reality and law". And on November 10th:[35]

"On November 12, the German people as a whole will choose *its* future. This future is bound to the Fuhrer. In choosing this future, the people cannot, on the basis of so-called foreign policy considerations, vote *Yes* without also including in the Yes the Fuhrer and the political movement that has pledged itself unconditionally to him."

More widely distributed (and internationally read) was Heidegger's inaugural address as rector on May 27, 1934, where he explicitly embraces the well-known Nazi

---

[35] Both quotes found in Chapter 2, "Political Texts 1933-1945", in ibid. of Wolin (1993).

phrases Volk, race, and soil:[36]

"And the spiritual world of a Volk is not its cultural superstructure, just as little as it is its arsenal of useful knowledge and values; rather, it is the power that comes from preserving at the most profound level the forces that are rooted in the soil and blood of a Volk, the power to arouse most inwardly and to shake most extensively the Volk's existence."

He also ominously proclaimed in his address, "The much praised "academic freedom" is being banished from the German university; for this freedom was false".

To all observers, the Nazis had found a fellow traveler.

01/13/2024

Karl Lowith writes of his last meeting with Heidegger in 1936 in Rome:[37]

"Even on this occasion, Heidegger did not remove the Party insignia from his lapel...it had obviously not occurred to him that the swastika was out of place while he was spending the day with me...I was of the opinion that his partisanship for National Socialism lay in the essence of his philosophy. Heidegger agreed with me

---

[36] Chapter 1, ibid. Wolin (1993).

[37] Wolin (1993), Chapter 7.

without reservation and added that his concept of "historicity" was the basis of his political engagement. He also left no doubt his belief in Hitler...To my response that one didn't have to be especially "refined" in order to renounce working with someone like Streicher, he answered: one need not waste words over Streicher, *Der Sturmer* was nothing more than pornography."

Lowith captures Heidegger's contradictions. A student of Heidegger whose work about his master helped launch his career, he had to emigrate from Germany despite being a Christian due to his Jewish descent. As others (Hannah Arendt, Hans Jonas, Herbert Marcuse, Leo Strauss) would testify, Heidegger's anti-Semitism was not personal; his was far from the visceral hate of Rosenberg or Streicher. He is known to have had affairs with Jewish women, the two most famous being Hannah Arendt and Elisabeth Blochmann, with both of whom he maintained a long-term correspondence (a correspondence interrupted unsurprisingly but poignantly by the Nazi years).

Heidegger's eclipse in 1934 and subsequent retreat from political activity allow his defenders to point to his time as rector as an aberration, like Plato's foray at Syracuse;[38] a reclamation Heidegger cultivated after the war. For others, it was less his activity during the Nazi years itself, reproachable as that was, than his

---

[38] Hannah Arendt, "Martin Heidegger at Eighty", *New York Review of Books*, October 21, 1971; Hans-Georg Gadamer, "Back from Syracuse", *Critical Inquiry* 15, 2 (1989).

subsequent silence about the Holocaust that is damning.[39] Derrida finds ways to excuse this silence. My undergraduate professor, Dominick LaCapra, chastises this exculpation.[40]

We now understand this silence. In 2014, the first volumes of *The Black Notebooks*, Heidegger's private journals from 1931-1969 were published. Heidegger had wanted the journals to be published. They reflect his thoughts, his works in progress. He thought they would be illuminating, a guide; a guide that only future generations would understand.

We do.

What the Black Notebooks reveal is that Heidegger remained a co-traveler with the Nazis for the entire duration of the regime. And that after the war his silence on the Shoah reflected a German chauvinism indifferent to the killings of Jews except as a propaganda tool to highlight the injustices he viewed being suffered by a defeated Germany. The analogies are grotesque and clarify one of the two public statements to come out of Heidegger about the Holocaust after the war in an exchange of letters with Herbert Marcuse in 1948 that

---

[39] George Steiner, *Martin Heidegger* (University of Chicago Press, 1978), p123f; Philippe Lacoue-Labarthe, ibid., p116; Jean-Francois Lyotard, *Heidegger and "the jews"*, translated by Andreas Michel and Mark Roberts (University of Minnesota Press, 1990) p4, 52.

[40] Dominick LaCapra, *Representing the Holocaust*, (Cornell University Press, 1994) p144f where one can find Derrida's excuses quoted.

an upset Marcuse would publish:[41]

"To the just and serious charges that you express about a regime that murdered millions of Jews, that made terror into an everyday phenomenon, and that turned everything that pertains to the ideas of spirit, freedom, and truth into its bloody opposite, I can merely add that of "Jews" you had written "East Germans" [i.e., Germans of the eastern territories, *statt "Juden" "Ostdeutsche"*], then the same holds true [*genauso*] for one of the Allies, with the difference that everything that has occurred since 1945 has become public knowledge, while the bloody terror of the Nazis in point of fact had been kept a secret from the German people."

There is a parcel of truth in Heidegger's statement, that Stalin's crimes were comparable to Hitler's. The gulags received a large new infusion of inmates after the war, mostly of Soviet origin (mostly Russian soldiers who like Solzhenitsyn's main crime was having seen the West). How many were "East Germans" is unclear, but Marcuse's response suggests that as of 1948 that

---

[41] Wolin (1993) Chapter 9. The second instance was in a lecture in Bremen in 1949 where he callously, cryptically equates the Holocaust with, amongst other things, the loss of our humanity's contact with the land: "Agriculture is now a mechanical food industry, in essence the same [das Selbe] as the production of corpses in the gas chambers and extermination camps, the same [das Selbe] as the blockading and starving of countries, the same [das Selbe] as the production of hydrogen bombs." Taken from Donatella Di Cesare, *Heidegger and the Jews: The Black Notebooks*, translated by Murtha Baca (Polity Press, 2018), p187.

number was considered small: "Even further: how is it possible to equate the torture, the maiming, and the annihilation of millions of men with the forcible relocation of population groups who suffered none of these outrages?". More important is that Heidegger only mentions "East Germans". If the point is to highlight the inhumanity of Stalin's regime, then what about the Holodomor, the engineered death of millions by famine in the Ukraine in the 1930s; or the purges of the latter 1930s; or simply the tens of millions incarcerated and destroyed by the gulags? The sole focus on "East Germans" is damning. Nor is Heidegger's claim that the terror of the Nazis was kept a secret plausible. The point of terror is not to be a secret. Where after all, did all the Jews, their hitherto neighbors, go? And if ignorance is possibly plausible, as implausible as that might be, to the general public, it is surely not acceptable for a leading thinker self-proclaimed devoted to questioning as was Heidegger.

01/14/2024

I will focus on the Black Notebooks and eschew other possible sources as these latter can be claimed to be marred. There are some notorious lectures in the 1930s (e.g., *Introduction to Metaphysics*, *The History of Being*) whose content Heidegger has argued must be deciphered due to the presence of Nazi enthusiasts in the audience.[42] And there are letters to his wife and

---

[42] In Heidegger's Letter to the Rector of Freiburg University, November 4, 1945; and the Der Spiegel interview from 1966, "Only a God Can Save Us",

brother that have become available that will be likewise skipped over, allowing that private utterances might reflect personal weaknesses not intended for public consumption. The Black Notebooks however were intended for publication and written without fears of official reprisal. The views found there are damnable and indicate that the distortions in these other sources are minimal. As the volume of material is significant (over three thousand pages thus far) and in German, I rely on two excellent books for culled translations, the first by Donatella Di Cesare, *Heidegger and the Jews*, originally released in 2014, and the second by Richard Wolin, *Heidegger in Ruins*, from 2023.[43] The tales they tell are consistent, and although containing significant overlap, there are differences in emphasis and original material quoted.

Consistent with his public lectures, Heidegger articulates an extreme German chauvinism, arguing for the unique historical and current philosophical role of Germany:[44]

"only someone who is German [der Deutsche] is capable of poetically articulating Being in an originary

published after his death and only after Heidegger's review and approval. Both can be found in Wolin (1993). The former was part of Heidegger's efforts to get reinstated after the war. The latter, one of the many efforts of some to whitewash Germany's past and personal culpability. One of the two interviewers, Georg Wolff, had been an officer in the SS.

[43] Richard Wolin, *Heidegger in Ruins: Between Philosophy and Ideology* (Yale University Press, 2023).

[44] Quotations from the Black Notebooks found in Wolin (2022) will be indicate by a "w", those from Di Cesare (2018), by a "d", followed by the page number.

way." [w4]

"The metaphysics of Dasein must, in accordance with its inner structure, deepen itself and be extended to the *metapolitics of the historical Volk*." [w57]

Jews are not only incapable of this greatness but its overt enemy:

"In the era of the Christian West—i.e., the era of metaphysics—*world Jewry is the principle of destruction*. "[w5]

"world Jewry...a human type...whose world-historical goal is the uprooting of all beings from Being" [w17]

"The more primordial and original [*ursprunglicher und anfanglicher*] future decisions and questions become, the more inaccessible they remain for this "race"." [w58]

"The question of the role of *world-Judaism* [Weltjudentum] is not a racial question, but a metaphysical [metaphysische] one, a question that concerns the kind of human existence which in an *utterly unrestrained* way can undertake as a world-historical "task" the uprooting of all beings from being." [d80]

"The occasional increase in the power of Judaism is grounded in the fact that Western metaphysics, especially in its modern evolution, offered the point of attachment for the expansion of an otherwise empty rationality and calculative capacity, and these thereby created for themselves an abode in the "spirit" without ever being able, on their own, the concealed decisive domains." [d78]

"The "victor" in this "struggle", which contests goallessness pure and simple and which can therefore only be the caricature of a "struggle", is perhaps the greatest groundlessness that, not being bound to anything, avails itself of everything (Judaism)." [d98]

"Even the thought of an agreement with England, in this sense of a division of the imperialistic "franchises", does not touch the essence of the historical process which England is now playing out to the end within Americanism and Bolshevism and thus at the same time with world-Judaism." [d161]

Despite his purported philosophical perspective, Heidegger is found to echo typical Nazi propaganda rationalizing the treatment of their victims:

"With their emphatically calculative giftedness, the Jews have for the longest time been "living" with the principle of race, which is why they are also offering the most vehement resistance to its unrestricted application. The instituting of racial breeding stems not from "life" itself, but from the over-powering of life by machination. What machination pursues with such planning is a complete deracializing of peoples through their being clamped into an equally built and equally

61

tailored instituting of all beings. One with the deracializing is a self-alienation of all the peoples—the loss of history, i.e., the loss of the domains of decision regarding beying." [d104]

"World Judaism, incited by the emigrants allowed out of Germany, cannot be held fast anywhere and, with all its developed power, does not need to participate anywhere in the activities of war, whereas all that remains to us is the sacrifice of the best blood of the best of our own people." [d154]

"One of the stealthiest forms of Gigantism [das Riesiege] and perhaps the most ancient, is the fast-paced *cleverness of calculation, huckstering, and intermingling*...whereby [world] Jewry's *worldlessness* is established." [w82]

When writing just after the war, Heidegger grotesquely argues that the Nazi extermination was abstractly a self-inflicted annihilation:

"Only when what is essentially "Jewish" in the metaphysical sense struggles against what is "Jewish", is the apex of self-annihilation in history reached. The condition is that what is "Jewish" has everywhere completely taken over domination so that even the struggle—and that first and foremost—against what is "Jewish" becomes subject to that." [d201]

In defeat, Germany's loss is lamented, victimhood concocted and histrionically, sinisterly, equated with a death camp and other crimes of the Nazis:

"The terror created by the final nihilism is even more horrific than all of the savagery of the executioners and of the concentration camps [Kz]." [d207]

"Is not the *failure to acknowledge* this destiny [*Geschick*], and repressing our *world-willing* [*Weltwollen*], a "fault", and an even more essential collective guilt whose enormity cannot be measured against the horror of the "gas chambers" ["*Gaskammern*"], a guilt more terrible than all the officially censurable, publicly "stigamatizable" "crimes" for which no one will apologize in future? It can already be perceived that the German people and the German territory are a single concentration camp [*ein einziges Kz*] such as the world has never seen and never wants to see, a not wanting much more willed and consensual than our *absence of will* in the face of the feralization of national socialism?" [d208]

"The true defeat is not in the fact that the "Reich" was destroyed, cities shattered, human beings killed by means of invisible death machines, but rather in the fact that the Germans are letting themselves be led toward self-annihilation of their own essence and that they are carrying this out with their own hands with the apparently plausible motive of eliminating that reign of terror that "Nazism" purportedly was." [d205]

"the destruction of Europe, however it may be achieved, with or without Russia, is the work of the

Americans. 'Hitler' is only a pretext." [d211]

"The *worldwide scandal that threatens* the German people, the scandal before the world that is hidden by their destiny—not before the "world" understood as a journalistic organization of public opinion--, is not in any way the "guilt" that is imputed to them, but rather their incapacity to immerse themselves in the purpose assigned to them by destiny, scorning the "world" of modernity." [d212]

What we find in the Black Notebooks and Heidegger's previously quoted proclamations, is: an elitist, an unrepentant enemy of liberal western values; a believer in a strong leader; a German chauvinist; an anti-Semite who targeted Jews as scapegoats.

In short: a Nazi.

Again

So, Heidegger was a fascist, Heisenberg a collaborator; so, what? Ironically Heisenberg, never the true believer, never a co-traveler, likely had more impact on history, by rallying the vast community of the world's physicists, those originally found outside and those that escaped the Reich, onto the Manhattan Project. If that is, one can minimize the importance that Heidegger's prestige, and those like him, lent Hitler in the Nazi's initial coalescence of power.

Heisenberg's status as one of the great scientists is secure; every student of modern physics learns of his work. The separation of the man, his politics, his ethics, whatever they, in fact, were from the achievement is complete; part of the nature of the field, the endeavor. With Heidegger, we are not so sure.

Richard Wagner was an anti-Semite and, the author of a scandalous screed.[45] Nevertheless, Mahler and Schoenberg both acknowledged his critical influence. Music is sufficiently abstract, and technical; like physics or mathematics. I can enjoy Wagner: in small doses. Eventually, the storylines, the glorification of Germany's ancient, bellicose gods, and the death romance--all that entranced Hitler--becomes too much. Eventually, the music itself is too much.

There is a long line of anti-Semitism in Western,

---

[45] Richard Wagner, *Judaism in Music* (1850). Heisenberg's chauvinism for German philosophy is mirrored in Wagner's claims regarding Music: "So long as the separate art of Music had a real organic life-need in it, down to the epochs of Mozart and Beethoven, there was nowhere to be found a Jew composer: it was impossible for an element entirely foreign to that living organism to take part in the formative stages of that life. Only when a body's inner death is manifest, do outside elements win the power of lodgment in it—yet merely to destroy it. Then indeed that body's flesh dissolves into a swarming colony of insect-life: but who, in looking on that body's self would hold it still for living? The spirit, that is: the *life*, has fled from out that body, has sped to kindred other bodies; and this is all that makes out Life. In genuine Life alone can we, too, find again the ghost of Art, and not within its worm-befretted carcase." (translation William Ashton Ellis). Historically, Wagner's relationship with the composer Meyerbeer, a Jew and an early benefactor, eerily echoes Heidegger's relationship with Husserl.

particularly Germanic, philosophy.[46] Do these exculpate Heidegger in any way? As a potential influence, they perhaps help situate his development. Like most of the great German philosophers, Heidegger was raised with strong Lutheran influences. The late Martin Luther was famously a vicious anti-Semite.[47] In his work on religion, Kant, to his ignorance and discredit, states that:[48]

"Strictly speaking, Judaism is not a religion at all but simply the union of a number of individuals who, since they belonged to a particular stock, established themselves into a community under purely, political laws, hence not into a church…"

I have trouble reconciling Kant as an anti-Semite with the author of the Categorical Imperative; who praised *Jerusalem*, Moses Mendelsohn's famous work that called for religious freedom; who as a young man changed his name from Emanuel to Immanuel after learning Hebrew; or with the author who promoted moral purity to the point of famously advocating that telling a lie is always wrong, even to an intended murderer.[49] Perhaps Kant's remarks on Judaism are a

---

[46] Augustine and Voltaire are two of the most famous, non-German, influential anti-Semites in the Western canon.

[47] Martin Luther, On Jews and their Lies, found in *The Essential Luther*, translated by Tryntje Hefferich (Hackett Publishing Company, 2018).

[48] Immanuel Kant, *Religion within the Boundaries of Mere Reason*, translated by George di Giovanni (Cambridge University Press, 2018) p154 (6:126).

[49] Immanuel Kant, *On the Supposed Right to Lie from Benevolent Motives*, 1797 essay. Thomas Kingsmill Abott's translation can be found online at http://www.sophia-project.org/uploads/1/3/9/5/13955288/kant_lying.pdf.

reflection of age, a decline in his powers. Perhaps, alternatively, it reflects an inherent inflexibility that crosses over to intolerance when morality is based solely on reason, without any admixture of compassion. Either way, Kant certainly added to a pre-existing anti-Semitic climate. The young Hegel, before his ascent in his own day to the pinnacle of German philosophy, expounded views resembling those of Luther.[50] The fact that the elder Hegel never denounced these earlier views is significant and must thus be taken to express his continued prejudices. Heidegger would certainly have known them. Nietzsche, with his writings on the overman, and the pernicious influence of moral ressentiment that he traced back to Judaism, is often viewed as the intellectual predecessor of the Nazis. He was certainly claimed as such by them. But this would be a distortion. Nietzsche was an elitist, an aristocrat, disgusted by humanity generally, who loathed not only democracy but also any form of collective pride. About Germans, he scathingly writes:[51]

"look at German taste, at German arts and manners what boorish indifference to "taste"! ...The German DRAGS at his soul, he drags at everything he experiences. He digests his events badly... And just as all chronic invalids, all dyspeptics like what is convenient, so the German loves "frankness" and "honesty"; it is so

---

[50] G. W. F. Hegel, Positivity of Christian Religion, found in *Early Theological Writings*, translated by T. M. Knox (University of Chicago Press, 1948).

[51] Friedrich Nietzsche, *Beyond Good and Evil*, translated by Helen Zimmern (1913), available online, 244.

CONVENIENT to be frank and honest...we should do honor to our name—we are not called the "TIUSCHE VOLK" (deceptive people) for nothing..."

And of the prejudices of his day:[52]

"among present-day Germans there is alternately the anti-French folly, the anti-Semitic folly, the anti-Polish folly, the Christian-romantic folly, the Wagnerian folly, the Teutonic folly, the Prussian folly (just look at those poor historians, the Sybels and Treitschkes, and their closely bandaged heads), and whatever else these little obscurations of the German spirit and conscience may be called."

That Nietzsche was nevertheless vigorously adopted by the Nazis might be less a reflection on him than an observation that authors, to paraphrase Sartre, are condemned to be read.

01/15/2024

Heidegger is reprehensible. He differs from his inheritance by events. A difference he was too weak, too small to confront; particularly after the war. Philosophy is not physics or mathematics, not when avoiding the minutia, not when done on the grand level. And Heidegger worked on the grand level. Like music, we hear the full man. Here is the disappointment, the

---

[52] Nietzsche, ibid., 251

disgust, the possibilities betrayed.

In the end is the beginning. For over fifty years there was no abrupt discontinuity in Heidegger's thought. The Shoah is absent, not just because it cannot be confronted, fitted into his framework,[53] but because for Heidegger it was simply not a concern. This is the clarity brought to us by the Black Notebooks. A clarity we owe to the victims: past and present.

Born of the Holocaust, Israel has seen its specter return this October, in all of its unvarnished hate. Bringing a unity, a determination, a clarity that even a Netanyahu cannot diminish.

The end we know is but one possible. History is not science;[54] Hitler was not inevitable. Those inspired by Heidegger need not be fascists. The French existentialists fought the Nazis. To deny that they're worth reading is flippant. So too with deconstruction

---

[53] Di Cesare summarizes this view well: "If Heidegger had discovered the singularity of Auschwitz, if he had recognized it as a traumatic event, he would have allowed that trauma to shatter the ontological coordinates, blowing the History of Being to smithereens. But on his nocturnal horizon, marked by a distant light that should illuminate the earth in the morning, no ontic intrusion could interrupt that destination—not even the eclipse of humanity." Ibid., p188. It was my perspective too (unacceptable as it is regarding Heidegger), not nearly as well articulated, more intuited, *prior* to the Black Notebooks.

[54] For a discussion that history as a truly predictive science would be inconsistent, see chapter 4, Joseph Milana, *On Hope and Knowledge: A Skeptics Reply and Other Reflections* (Archway, 2018).

(though perhaps less so), however incoherent.[55] Heidegger will continue to be read. Ought to be read; only in full. For the shadow cast; for the aspiration; for the monstrosity.

That clarity too.

Emmanuel Levinas, another inheritor of the tradition that spawned Heidegger, who, in his magnus opus *Totality and Infinity* combined it with another, his Jewish inheritance, wrote of Heidegger:[56]

"One can forgive many Germans, but there are some Germans it is difficult to forgive. It is difficult to forgive Heidegger."

I do not know how redemption is possible, all the Anne Franks lost, but I do know forgiveness must first be sought, must first be asked. Heidegger never did; nor did Heisenberg.

By whom, from Whom, Of Whom?

Again, no answer.

But after Auschwitz, after October 7th, this clarity too: it needs seeking.

01/16/2024

---

[55] See chapter 5 of Milana, ibid., for an elaboration that Derrida's flight from logic is a fatal flaw, allowing any utterance be argued.

[56] Emmanuel Levinas, *Nine Talmudic Readings*, translated Annette Aronowicz (Indiana University Press, 1990) p25.

3
KADDISH

Today we attended our third funeral this week. Linda died suddenly of a dissecting aneurism in the aorta, one week after her daughter's wedding; all of 59. Mike and I worked together at HNC: my first landing station after being jettisoned from Physics. We were part of a monthly wine-tasting group. They crashed in our backyard, having thrown up a pair of tents, along with Elba and Levent, after Lauren's 50th gala, (our house was already full with family). I had drawn close to Levent and Mike after the Sumitomo crisis: Mike on sight in Japan; me back here in San Diego working around the clock with Arati to resolve the software bug; all eyes upon us, the CEOs of both companies requiring daily updates. We hadn't seen much of Linda or Mike lately, since they retired and moved to Indiana to be near her parents. Where her funeral is being held. We'll be in San Diego, watching online over Zoom. One of the fixtures from the Covid years.

The first funeral, another Zoom event in Chicago, was for the father of a friend we've known since DC, since Becky was a toddler; Lauren and Denise being part of a new Mom's group along with their eldest, Josh. We last saw Denise and John this summer when driving across the country. John, being a doctor, was then absorbed in his father's care; as he had been for the last couple of years. The trajectory was clear. More than the physical, the mental diminishment (from medication, lack of care previously, or what) is the hardest. He had lived a long life; in the end, we're shocked to call what it is, a relief. And a restoration, in memory, in this release, of the vibrant man he once was: the son's hero; as it was with my own father.

12/21/2023

And then there's Ben. The 31-year-old son of friends, more very good acquaintances, from Temple. Just one year older than Becky. Natural causes we're told. What started as a stomach ailment two days earlier; living alone in Colorado (the State of his mother's birth and upbringing, home still to his grandparents), where he had recently become the music instructor at Ponderosa High School in Parker CO, after graduating with his Masters from the Jacob's School of Music in Bloomington, Indiana (again Indiana). The funeral was held here in San Diego, his body having been flown home. Hundreds in attendance; the size, following the rule of funerals, inversely related to the age of the departed.

Three funerals: one acceptable, in the flow, the embrace of mortality, the reciprocal of the miracle of birth no parent or grandparent would wish to deny. One too soon, for all the love that remained to be given. And one a tragedy; every parent's nightmare; always in the background, too horrible to acknowledge, never mind speak out loud.

(12/23/2023)

This outrage, this indignation. Not Defiance, no, not that, yet a refusal at placid submission. Towards this home, our World, not Home. In its mirror, in confidence, in an insistence yet a dependence, acknowledged, known, in it a hint of something more: Righteousness.

Not a proof, for sure; not even convincing, yet, yet for all that, perhaps persuasive nevertheless.

If only.   (01/02/2024)

After Ben's funeral, that very day, off to the doctor's for my ten-year renewal of TDAP, the whooping cough vaccine (amongst others) to protect Laura's infant son.

It is what must be done.

                                        12/21/2023

APPENDIX

of remembrances of letting go, this not letting go.

Farewell to Dimpy

(08/11/2011)

Dimpy

If Anu is playing this audio, I am assuming it is because it is the last time I'll have to talk to you. That makes me very sad. You have enriched our lives. Professionally, you've made those you've worked with better: one of the lasting impacts you've had on me is that when I now encounter a new problem, I'll ask what would Dimpy think? And if I feel I could satisfy your review, I know I've solved the problem. Of everyone I've worked with since coming to San Diego 15 years ago, you have been my favorite collaborator, my favorite colleague; a good friend. You're leaving behind friends who will miss you and a family that loves you: a life well lived I'd say. Regarding your daughter, I promise that as she grows up, I'll help Rita know who her mother was. And if you'll indulge me, here's my Hope: a hope not yet faith, yet from embracing Uncertainty, that all this will somehow make sense, somehow balance out, and that this is just a pause in our friendship.

With all my love, Joe.

My words at Dad's Funeral

(01/15/2012)

We meet today with a Heavy heart, and as we wrestle with the Hole that's formed in our lives, I take some solace in an observation that my Sister made: that we should remember that my father lived a long life, longer than any other Milana. No other Milana had lived until 80, never mind nearly 90. His life was full, he died peacefully at home, surrounded by family. For this, we should be grateful. I am 50, Dad only had his father until he was 35. For this I am grateful.

A "Problem" I used to think about when I was a kid: If you met someone in Heaven, what would they look like?

Over the course of a long life, we're many people, known in many different ways; as the bard says, many "acts". So, who would be in Heaven, how would we appear to all those we've known?

Sometime later I arrived at a "solution" I found acceptable: you see those you know in the Image as you knew them.

For those who only know my father from these last few years in San Diego, I have Two images of Dad:

1) As a kid of ~ 13: more or less my current age.

Active, a forceful presence; a mix of the ex-marine

and the smartest person I knew growing up. Excelled in everything he put his mind to:

1) an ex-Marine, marksman, who said he hit what he shot at, and in battle shot often

2) Master of Chem Engineering (finishing 5 yr. program in 4) and champion swimmer,

3) who also studied and even for a while practiced, psychoanalysis.

4) Who could smash a golf ball over 300 yards;

5) a bowler loved to compete; Sunday morning gambling. Particularly special as Uncle Victor would also go, and come back to the house.

6) Who had a photographic memory, something I only understood later (drive in the car).

7) And a salesman who would yell on the phone at his customers, call them stupid: they came to him because he solved their problems.

Dad didn't believe in conventions.

He valued his independence: If you don't like the rules, change them.

Like how we modified the rules to Scrabble to reduce the impacts of chance.

The story he would like to tell was the first time he took me to work: traveled around to clients. Would be back by lunch so he could play a round of golf (valued his time > money). I asked, so Dad, when do you begin work? He explained some people work with their heads, some with their backs. And that's a lesson that left a strong imprint.

2) As a young man. He explained that during childhood, there are lots of dynamics involved between a father and son, but once you grow up, a father becomes more like a friend.

So down in the lab he had in our home (where he supported his sales of textile dyes with formulas of how to use the dyes), we'd talk about career choices, people, and philosophy. Over the past handful of years, I missed that friend the most.

We'd get glimmers of that person; sometime while playing scrabble, or, before this last trip to Asia, told him I was going to visit India and China. He related to the excitement of foreign travel, but heeded me, "Don't do anything stupid". This resonated, as he had once told me that the one reason he survived Guadalcanal was that he had never done anything crazy/stupid. When I was on Hua-shan...

Dad enjoyed life but was not afraid of death. Stated with his usual self-assurance, that when he died, he would talk to God about all that was wrong in this world. Over the years I appreciated that this was not a literary use, of the term. He believed there was a creator, there was more than what met the eye. And, perhaps starting from his days as a marine, that his life was graced. And this is perhaps the last lesson he has to teach us all.

Goodbye Dad, we'll miss you.

Provided for Bill's Funeral

(03/27/2021)

So much of this feels wrong. A funeral for a man Bill's age, a man preceding most of his contemporaries, would typically be packed, by all those he loved and loved him; friends and family. So Covid changing that is wrong. And of course, his death itself, the cancer, feels wrong. But most importantly, when I think about Bill, it's this sorrow, this loss that feels wrong. Bill was always so much fun, always someone I looked forward to and enjoyed seeing. This grief, this sorrow, is what's incongruous.

I recall, when we were kids and he and Amy came to New York, the excitement of seeing Bill. The first thing he would do, when we went off together, was head to the nearest candy store and fill up a big bag with candy: mounds, snickers, M&Ms, Starbursts, Kit-Kats, anything he could get his hands on. And he would have me promise not to tell Aunt Natalie or Uncle Dick. We would then share a few candy bars, stuffing our mouths. The rest he'd sneak back with him into our house for later consumption. And sure enough, within a day or two, we would be going back to that candy store.

And over the years, that's what seeing Bill was always like. One big bag of candy. I am so, so grateful to have known Bill. There was always laughter when he was around. My sometimes slipping into calling him "Billy", and him calling me "Joey". One of the only people for whom that was OK.

That's how I am sure he'd want us to remember him. And how he'd want us to carry on: not with overwhelming sorrow, stifling grief, but by sharing stories, recalling the good times, the laughter, the joy we had together. I am so, so grateful to have known him.

My words at Mom's Funeral

(09/17/2021)

My mother passed over two weeks ago, after spending over a year in hospice care. Wherever she is now, it's in a better place than where she has been. And as time continues to pass, I am getting more and more of my mother back.

Over the course of her long life, she played in my life many parts: a great-grandmother, a grandmother, mother-in-law, confidant. Yet what I think of most, when she meant most to me, was as a young child. The greatest gift a parent can give their children is to know that they are loved. My father, having practiced for a while as a psychoanalyst, knew this. My mother lived this every day. She nurtured and loved unconditionally. Always supportive, never judgmental. My brother Richard can't be here today due to the current dangers of traveling (Hi Rich). Born with special needs, he has lived happily in a group home in New Jersey for upwards of 40 years. It was my mother's extraordinary efforts that integrated him into society. Loved & loving, I don't know if she understood how good a mother she was.

She was also a teacher. I'll tell a story I told at her 90th birthday celebration but that I think is worth retelling. Growing up, my grandmother, my mother's father, lived with us. My mother used to say that all of my father's worst traits came from his mother. My grandmother would do her own grocery shopping, walking to the Waldbaum's less than a ½ mile from our home. Often, I would go with her. She was a small woman, less than 5' tall, and weighed less than 100 pounds. When we'd get to the deli counter, there was often a line, sometimes very crowded. This was before the time of tickets and counters. So, what did my grandmother do? Step in line? NO, she would take my hand and say "Come on", and would slip and push her way to the front of the line, raise her hand, cutting everyone, and immediately start to order. As a boy, I was embarrassed and ashamed. When I'd recount the episode to my mother, she was livid and explained that this was why she would not take my grandmother shopping. She said that it wasn't just that the behavior was embarrassing, but, with emphasis, that it was wrong.

During the inversion of the last few weeks, when instead of immediately burying my mother, we were clearing out her room at the Remington, I felt at times that as we packed up her things & the place emptied, she was being erased. Her presence gone. Such are the clouds of grief. And terribly, foolishly wrong, I realize now, for she'll always be right here, with us. I love you, Mom. Thank you.

With his permission, Daniel's words at Miriam's Funeral

(10/10/2023)

Hi everybody and thanks for being here. We'll be having a memorial ceremony for Mim where family and friends will be able to share their memories, but I wanted to share a few thoughts here with you today about how I'll remember my sister.

What stands out to me most is her smile, which could lighten up a room, and her laughter, which was infectious. Many of you may have seen her comedy shows. But the two of us could amuse each other almost anytime, anywhere, sometimes with arch observations, but mostly with funny voices and stupid jokes. Much of the time, we were the only ones who understood each other, and no occasion was too sacred, like the time I mentioned at the end of a meeting with her oncologist that I almost left the office disappointed, and Mim immediately knew that it was because we had to wait until the end of the session for the doctor to say "co-LON" in her Irish accent. We were cracking up all the way down the elevator.

Mim was a joyous singer. I think she knew the lyrics to every Beatles song and singing them together was another thing that we shared. But that only scratched the surface. Her repertoire extended as far as gospel music, Tom Jones, Peggy Lee, and beyond. Most recently, she started singing cabaret. At any minute she was liable to finish a song that she might have heard a snippet of on TV or in the street. But I'm not sure she ever appreciated the irony that Mom, another epic singer, could drive us both crazy doing something very similar.

My sister was also a visual artist and her color could fill a painting the way that her smile filled a room. I particularly loved her pastel watercolors, which look a bit like Mondrian, only better. To me, they showed a balance, harmony, and repose that may have eluded her in life. They have delighted and inspired me to do a bit of my own dabbling in photography which, to be clear, doesn't approach the same level. I'm so grateful that she left these treasures behind for me and the rest of her loved ones to enjoy and remember her by.

Jessicka, Mim's friend and caregiver, recently told me how unusual it was that all three of the Nelson children, Miriam, my brother David and me, were spiritual seekers. For some reason, I'd never thought about that, but it's indisputably true. In Mim's case, while she retained a Jewish identity, she had several teachers who had a great impact on her and she made several trips to India to study with two of them, the Hindu guru Sathya Sai Baba and Zen master Dolano. Unfortunately, after she got diagnosed and had to confront her own mortality, these teachings weren't as much of a comfort as she might have hoped. She became a lot more focused on what she could feel and experience in the here and now. And she didn't want any type of cleric to officiate at her funeral, telling us, and this will go down as a classic Mim line, "I don't want anybody who thinks they know more than I do". Even in the hardest of circumstances, things were best expressed through the lens of humor.

I think most of you who are here know that Mim's relationship with her family wasn't easy. Part of me was hoping, naively, that before she passed, we'd be able to have the Hollywood moment and resolve all issues and grievances in a loving embrace. Unfortunately, that didn't happen. I'm not sure it ever really does, and by the time Mim was ready to acknowledge that she was nearing the end, her physical decline was pretty rapid and it wasn't possible anyway. But I do want to say that she deeply loved her family and was deeply loved by them. I know that the presence of Mom, my wife Solange, our cousin Joe, and me at the end was a comfort to her and I'm glad we were able to ease her passage a bit.

Her relationship with her dogs was a lot less complicated. Isn't that true for a lot of us? She had two shi-tzus. Bhakti, who died about 6 years ago, and Hamilton, who's here today. Some of you might also remember Lucy, who she had when she was living in Boston, of a similar size and shape, but unknown ethnicity. Mim was devoted to her dogs and would do anything for them. They reciprocated. One of my last fun memories of Mim is her laughing as Hamilton love-bombed her by licking her head, which she had shaved due to the radiation. By the end, we had to coax Hamilton to leave the house when it was time for a walk. He knew something was going on and I think he wanted to go through it with her.

The last thing I want to talk about is the devotion of Mim's caregivers. Solange was a constant presence and took off the better part of two weeks from work to give care and comfort to Mim and provide some needed respite to Jessicka. Mom's health aide, Donna, was also a source of comfort and support throughout Mim's illness. And thanks, also, to cousin Joe, for staying with Mim through that last crucial day. And then there is Mim's dear friend, Jessicka Chamberlin. Many people have good intentions, but far fewer of them really follow through. Jessicka is one of the second kind. When she found out that Mim's cancer had reached a decisive phase, Jessicka volunteered to come here from California and care for Mim through the whole cycle of her illness. She was true to her word and stayed with Mim through thick and thin, including some epic anxiety and downright crankiness on Mim's part. She's been a godsend and I can't thank her enough for her devotion to my dear sister.

Mim left us too soon and I'll miss her deeply, but I hope that we can appreciate what she shared with us in the time we had with her and celebrate the vivacious joy and vivid color that she brought to the world. As we say in the Jewish tradition (and I hope she'll forgive me for this), **zichrona livracha**, "may her memory be a blessing."

www.ingramcontent.com/pod-product-compliance
Lightning Source LLC
Chambersburg PA
CBHW051229120626
46547CB00013B/1564